GCSE REVISION NOTES ON PRIESTLEY'S AN INSPECTOR CALLS
- Study guide (All acts, page-by-page analysis)

by Joe Broadfoot

Copyright © Joe Broadfoot, 2015

The right of Joe Broadfoot to be identified as the author of this work has been asserted in accordance with Section 77 of the Copyright, Designs and Patents Act 1988

ISBN-13:
978-1514163429

ISBN-10:
151416342X

Brief Introduction

This book is aimed at iGCSE and GCSE students of English Literature who are studying J.B. Priestley's *An Inspector Calls*. The focus is on what examiners are looking for, especially since the changes to the curriculum in 2015, and here you will find relevant themes covered in detail. I hope this will help you and be a valuable tool in your studies and revision.

Criteria for high marks

Make sure you use appropriate critical language (see glossary of literary terms at the back). You need your argument to be fluent, well-structured and coherent. Stay focused!

Analyse and explore the use of form, structure and the language. Explore how these aspects affect the meaning.

Make connections between texts and look at different interpretations. Explore their strengths and weaknesses. Don't forget to use supporting references to strengthen your argument.

Analyse and explore the context.

Best essay practice

Use PEE for your paragraphs: point/evidence/explain.

Other tips

Make your studies active!

Don't just sit there reading! Never forget to annotate, annotate and annotate!

All page references refer to the 2000 edition of *An Inspector Calls and Other Plays* published by Penguin Classics (ISBN-13: 978-0-141-18535-4).

AQA (New specification starting in 2015)

If you're studying for an AQA qualification in English Literature, there's a good chance your teachers will choose this text to study. There are good reasons for that: it's moralistic and familiar to students. The text encourages us to think about right and wrong.

However, one of the difficulties is the language. That can't be helped, bearing in mind that part A of the exam paper involves answering questions on Shakespeare, whereas part B is all about the 19th-century novel.

To further complicate things, the education system is in a state of flux: that means we have to be ready for constant change. Of course, everyone had got used to grades A,B and C meaning a pass. It was simple, it was straightforward and nearly everyone understood it. Please be prepared that from this day henceforward, the top grade will now be known as 9. A grade 4 will be a pass, and anything below that will be found and anything above it will be a pass. Hopefully, that's not too confusing for anyone!

Now onto the exam itself. As I said, paper 1 consists of Shakespeare and the 19th-century novel. It is a written closed book exam (in other words you are not allowed to have the texts with you), which lasts one hour 45 minutes. You can score 64 marks, which amounts to 40% of your GCSE grade. The other 60% is gained from paper 2, which is all about modern texts, poetry and unseen poetry.

Of course, paper 2 is what we will focus on as *An Inspector Calls* is one of the texts listed under drama. The other choices include, Willy Russell's *Blood Brothers*, Alan Bennett's *The History Boys*, Dennis Kelly's *DNA*, Simon Stephens's play script of The Curious Incident of the Dog in the Night-time and Shelagh Delaney's *A Taste of Honey*.

For your information, the choice of prose texts has to be one of the following: William Golding's *Lord of the Flies* , the AQA Anthology entitled *Telling Tales* , George Orwell's *Animal Farm*, Kazuo Ishiguro's *Never Let Me Go* , Meera Syal's Anita and Me, or Steven Kelman's *Pigeon English*.

Additionally, students are expected to study a cluster of poems taken from the AQA Poetry Anthology entitled: *Poems Past and Present*. Each cluster contains 15 poems. Students can choose to study the cluster concerning love and relationships or they can concern themselves with power and conflict.

There will also be a section on the exam which involves writing on announcing poem. Students should revise by studying poetry in general and look to describe content, theme, structure and the use of language to secure the maximum marks.

Paper 2 is worth 60% (96 raw marks) of your GCSE, and most of the marks are gained from your ability to analyse language, form and structure (AO2). AO1 (which involves giving and supporting your informed opinion) is worth 22.5% (36 raw marks) of your GCSE, AO2 makes up 27.5% (44 raw marks), AO3 (context) is 7.5% (12 raw marks) and AO4 (spelling, punctuation, grammar and vocabulary) is 2.5% (4 raw marks).

An Inspector Calls is worth 34 raw marks including 2.5% (4 marks) for AO4. The other 62 raw marks on Paper 2 can be garnered from poetry analysis.

As you can see, we've got a lot to get through so without further ado let's get on it!

An Inspector Calls

iGCSE

J.B. Priestley's text is not necessarily one you'll encounter if you're doing iGCSE. However, I've noticed that it's recently become a popular choice of teachers, who are looking for something to engage students. *An Inspector Calls* generally does that and it also gives us plenty to debate, which may be why it is now being used for iGCSE coursework. Assignment 3 of the iGCSE course gives students a chance to write in response to an opinion. If you're going to do that, you need to write in a different format to most essays. Instead of being objective, as you should be in most academic essays, you should be subjective. In other words, you have to write in an opinionated way, using lines like: 'In my opinion'. Most students are good at that! Just don't make it a habit, as you should never forget that writing an iGCSE essay involves different skills to what you need with other exam boards.

If you're set an essay to complete for assignment 3 of your iGCSE coursework, the chances are it will be about notions of **collective responsibility** or **social responsibility**, which amounts to the same thing. I've seen questions that ask how Priestley's dramatises the words above (in bold) and, in answer to that question, the first thing I would do is draw four lines on a page, with the following sub-titles:

Evidence	Character's POV	JBP's POV	My POV

Then I would proceed to add notes beneath those sub-headings. For iGCSE, it is expected that students write between 8-10 paragraphs and between 500 and 800 words. Therefore I would be looking for at least 8 paragraph headings (which I would use for my initial notes, but delete when submitting the first draft). I would usually write more than that to start with and then cut out unnecessary or redundant sentences and phrases afterwards. You have to be ruthless with your editing: if you don't need something, cut it out!

The most common errors I've seen could mostly have been avoided. They come about because of students not proof-reading their work. Even the most intelligent ones are nbot immune, sometimes forgetting how to spell the playwright's name. Attention to detail is important. We all make mistakes, but please do your utmost to avoid them; it can make you look sloppy and send out all the wrong messages to the examiner, whom you want to impress.

Anyway, enough about that! Let's see how I would fare with the same question on social responsibility. I'll start with my notes.

Evidence	Character's POV	JBP's POV	My POV
1. 'There's a good deal of silly talk about […] I speak as a hard-headed business man […] ignore all this silly pessimistic talk'	AB is interested in business & money only. Portrayed as wealthy, without much concern for employees. Lacks a social conscience	Doesn't agree with Arthur Birling. Shows it through dramatic irony when Birling predicts a prosperous & peaceful future, before Great Depression & WW1. JBP's arguing in favour of collective responsibility	In my opinion, rich business people can become obsessed with making profit to the detriment of their workers.

OR

I think rich business pay a lot of taxes etc |

2. 'Just because the miners came out on strike...we employers are coming together...we're in for a time of steadily increasing prosperity'	AB is optimistic about the future. He believes that rich capitalists will prevail over their poorer workforce	Doesn't agree with AB. He makes him look ridiculous, as the General Strike of 1926 and the Great Depression that followed proved AB's predictions were wrong	Strikes do not appear to achieve very much, in my opinion. Many of the workers that went out on strike in 1926 lost their jobs thereafter or took a cut in wages and worked longer hours. No wonder there hasn't been a general strike since
3. 'the Titanic...every luxury and unsinkable, absolutely unsinkable'	AB's blind belief in progress is exemplified by this quotation. He believes in what he reads in the newspapers	The Titanic's spectacular demise may be symbolic, as it shows how foolhardy people in power can be. The captain of the ill-fated ship shouted 'Every man for himself', according to some accounts after his ship hit an iceberg. He was an	I believe belief has to be grounded in facts. It is always good to be sceptical of new developments

		upwardly mobile middle-class man, like AB. Smith was known as the 'millionaire's captain'	
4. 'let's say in 1940 – by that time you'll be living in a world that will have forgotten all about these Capital versus Labour agitations'	AB is convinced that future strife will be averted, when it comes to industrial disputes	As a committed socialist, clearly JBP would disagree	Although there haven't been any general strikes, there have been many industrial disputes since 1926, some of which have nearly brought the country to a standstill. It seems that some irresponsible business owners will always put profits before the welfare of their workers and this bound to lead to industrial action.
5. 'a man has to make his own way – has to look after himself – and his	AB believes a man should look after his family, but put himself first. He's a	Rather than believing in 'survival of the fittest', JBP wanted to	While family is important, equality is important. If we followed AB's

family too...these cranks talk...everybody has to look after everybody else (like) bees in a hive – community and all that nonsense	social Darwinist.	promote a more egalitarian and fairer society.	example the business world would be even more riddled with nepotism than it is.
6. 'I have an idea that your [Gerald's] mother - Lady Croft - while she doesn't object to my girl [Sheila] - feels you might have done better for yourself socially'	AB is feeling the effects of being nouveau riche as opposed to being born 'with a silver spoon in his mouth'	JBP is making the audience realise that even the prejudiced suffer discrimination sometimes	I think the class system still exists in British society and, although there is more upward and downward mobility nowadays, unfortunately prejudice on the basis of class is still with us
7. 'We can't let all these Bernard Shaws and H.G. Wellses do all the talking'	AB is attacking two prominent literary socialists	JBP is making the political battle lines clearer to the audience	We should listen to both sides of an argument before making our minds up, but AB's blustering form of conservatism is utterly unconvincing

8. 'They'll be peace and prosperity everywhere - except of course in Russia - which will always be behindhand, naturally'	AB's xenophobia and racism is apparent	JBP portrays AB as a bigot, whom it is almost impossible for the audience to sympathise with.	Xenophobia and racism are completely irrational. The only way to bring peace and prosperity to the world is by the elimination of negativity.

Now that I've come up with 8 quotations, I'm going to turn this into my first essay draft (without an introduction or a conclusion). Note that I won't start any paragraph with a quotation and I may well break them up into more manageable chunks.

1st draft

Paragraph 1 - hard-headed businessman?

Arthur Birling is interested in business and money mainly. He's portrayed as wealthy, without much concern for employees. He also seems to lacks a social conscience, but admits it, as he describes himself as 'a hard-headed businessman'. He is the eternal optimist, telling anyone who will listen to 'ignore all this silly pessimistic talk'. However, with World War One looming on the horizon in 1912 (when the play is set), there is a lot to be pessimistic about. Priestley is using dramatic irony to portray Birling as a buffoon and discredit his opinions. While it is difficult to condemn someone for being an optimist, it is not good to have a dreamer masquerading as a realist, as appears to be the case with Birling. In short, he is the type of character that gives business a bad name, as he's dim-witted rather than 'hard-headed'.

Paragraph 2 - miners

Indeed, Birling's predictions are continually lampooned through the use of dramatic irony. The audience has the benefit of hindsight and knows the error inherent in other Birling statements, such as: 'Just because the miners came out on strike, there's a lot of wild talk about possible labour trouble'. Priestley deliberately makes sure that Birling 'gets egg on his face', as most of the audience will know the General Strike of 1926 brought the country to a standstill just over a decade later. However, the strikers were not victorious ultimately, as many lost their jobs in the aftermath, or had to suffer longer hours or pay cuts. As much as Birling is ridiculed by the playwright, it is usually the business owners who win industrial disputes.

Paragraph 3 - Titanic

Although not quite as much a victim as impoverished pre-World War One workers, Birling is also a dupe. His blind belief in progress and the mass media is exemplified by his description of the Titanic as 'absolutely unsinkable'. No doubt many people in 1912 believed this to be true, shortly before the boat sank in April of that year. Priestley is showing how what the majority believe is not necessarily the truth and that we should question everything. It represents the failings of big business, who put profits before the safety of passengers. This, of course, led to a catastrophic loss of life when the doomed ship hit an iceberg as there were not enough lifeboats on board. Like Priestley, I believe that all lives are worth protecting, no matter what the cost.

Paragraph 4 - Social Darwinism

Interestingly, the captain of the aforementioned Titanic, Edward Smith, may have agreed with Birling on many issues, given his last words were reputed to be: 'every man for himself'. This sentiment is echoed in the play by Birling, who says: 'a man [...] has to look after himself – and his family too'. Birling believes in survival of the fittest, economically at least, judging by this quotation and his lack of sympathy for the plight of Eva Smith, later in the play. As a committed socialist, Priestley would have frowned on this type of individualism or Social Darwinism. Likewise, while I believe individuals must look after themselves, I don't think it should be to the detriment of others.

Paragraph 5 - social prejudice

Ironically, Birling himself is the victim of a similar kind of sentiment. While he has married into the upper classes, his offspring, Sheila, is still not considered the equal of Gerald Croft. Birling shows he is aware of the social disparity, when he says to Gerald: 'I have an idea that your mother - Lady Croft - while she doesn't object to my girl - feels you might have done better for yourself socially'. Priestley may not quite make the audience sympathise with Birling's character at this point, but at least the playwright shows us that even the prejudiced can be victims of discrimination. While that does not justify discriminatory behaviour, it makes one realise how class warfare can be perpetuated: Birling's desperation to be accepted by the aristocracy may have led to him distancing himself from the working classes.

Paragraph 6 - racism

Another form of prejudice rears its ugly head in the play, when Birling speaks of Russia. He clearly underestimates that nation's capabilities as he refers to them as 'behindhand, naturally'. He also prefaces that, by saying they will 'always' be that way. Birling is suggesting that Russia will be perpetually backward, and such a statement smacks of racism and xenophobia. Ironically, despite his belief in 'peace and prosperity' in years to come, attitudes like these can lead to warfare. Priestley shows the audience that Birling's prejudice knows no bounds, which makes him a truly unsympathetic character. If we want to make the world a safer and better place to live, we have to try eliminate all forms of prejudice from our hearts and minds.

Paragraph 7 - sexual discrimination

However, another form of prejudice exists within Birling, which manifests itself in the form of sexual discrimination. He tells Sheila that when she's married she'll 'realize that men with important work to do sometime have to spend nearly all their time and energy on business'. Ironically, Gerald, her fiancé, had been spending much of the last summer being unfaithful. Birling's words later take on a new resonance, as 'important work' becomes a euphemism for 'an affair'. Priestley, once again, makes the audience despise Birling's attitude; although Gerald's infidelity is yet to be revealed, at this stage. Although Birling also tells his daughter that she'll have to get used to it, her reply that she doesn't 'believe' she 'will' indicates her resistance to the dominant patriarchy. While I would commend her behaviour by 1912 standards, I would expect her to be much more outspoken in the face of sexual discrimination if it were to happen in a modern setting.

Paragraph 8 - ageism

Birling's condescending and patronising tone is not simply reserved for women: his children are also victims in that sense. The fact that he talks over them indicates he doesn't listen to their views. When Eric tries to speak early on in the play, Birling continues in the same dominant vein, telling him: 'You've a lot to learn yet'. Priestley later shows us the irony in that statement, as it's Birling and his wife who learn the least after the Inspector's call. Priestley belief that younger people have more capability to learn from their mistakes than older people is exemplified by the older Birlings comparative lack of remorse at the end of the play. Of course, I would like to see the next generation make less mistakes than the previous one, but I'm not sure that will happen unless we work hard to make sure it does.

Comments

Right then. I've completed the main body of the text, adding a couple of quotation that didn't feature in my plan. I just wanted the piece to flow and once I started writing about prejudice I ran with it. That made for clear paragraph headings, making it easier for me to switch gently from subject to subject. However, it's 1,125 words long. Oh no! A lot of editing needs to be done. Obviously, I'm going to get rid of the sub-titles, but I'm going to have to be ruthless. Let's go editing!

2nd draft

Arthur Birling seems to lack a social conscience, but admits it, as he describes himself as 'a hard-headed businessman'. He is the eternal optimist, telling anyone who will listen to 'ignore all this silly pessimistic talk'. However, with World War One looming on the horizon in 1912 (when the play is set), there is a lot of pessimism about. Priestley is using dramatic irony to portray Birling as a buffoon and discredit his opinions. In short, he is giving business a bad name, as he's dim-witted rather than 'hard-headed'.

Indeed, Birling's predictions are continually lampooned through the use of dramatic irony. The audience has the benefit of hindsight and know the error inherent in other Birling statements, such as: 'Just because the miners came out on strike, there's a lot of wild talk about possible labour trouble'. Priestley deliberately makes sure that Birling 'gets egg on his face', as most of the audience will know the General Strike of 1926 brought the country to a standstill just over a decade later. However, the strikers were not victorious ultimately, as many lost their jobs in the aftermath, or had to suffer longer hours or pay cuts. As much as Birling is ridiculed by the playwright, it is usually the business owners who win industrial disputes.

Although not quite as much a victim as impoverished pre-First World War workers, Birling is also a dupe. His blind belief in progress and the mass media is exemplified by his description of the Titanic as 'absolutely unsinkable'. For Priestley, it represents the failings of big business, who put profits before the safety of passengers. This, of course, led to a catastrophic loss of life when the doomed ship hit an iceberg as there were not enough lifeboats on board. Like Priestley, I believe that all lives are worth protecting, no matter what the cost.

Interestingly, the captain of the aforementioned Titanic, Edward Smith, may have agreed with Birling on many issues, given his last words were reputed to be: 'every man for himself'. This sentiment is echoed in the play by Birling, who says: 'a man [...] has to look after himself – and his family too'. Birling believes in survival of the fittest, economically at least, judging by this quotation. As a committed socialist, Priestley would have frowned on this type of individualism or Social Darwinism. Likewise, while I believe individuals must look after themselves, I don't think it should be to the detriment of others.

Ironically, Birling himself is the victim of a similar kind of sentiment. While he has married into the upper classes, his offspring, Sheila, is still not considered the equal of Gerald Croft. Birling's awareness of the social disparity is revealed, when he says to Gerald: 'I have an idea that your mother - Lady Croft - while she doesn't object to my girl - feels you might have done better for yourself socially'. Priestley may not quite make the audience sympathise with Birling's character at this point, but at least the playwright shows us that even the prejudiced can be victims of discrimination. While that does not justify discriminatory behaviour, it makes one realise how class warfare can be perpetuated: Birling's desperation to be accepted by the aristocracy may have led to him distancing himself from the working classes.

Another form of prejudice rears its ugly head in the play, when Birling speaks of Russia. He clearly underestimates that nation's capabilities as he refers to them as 'behindhand, naturally'. Priestley shows the audience that Birling's prejudice knows no bounds, which makes him a truly unsympathetic character. If we want to make the world a safer and better place to live, we have to try eliminate all forms of prejudice from our hearts and minds.

However, another form of prejudice exists within Birling, which manifests itself in the form of sexual discrimination. He tells Sheila that when she's married she'll 'realize that men with important work to do sometime have to spend nearly all their time and energy on business'. Ironically, Gerald, her fiancé, had been spending much of the last summer being unfaithful. Priestley, once again, makes the audience despise Birling's attitude; although Gerald's infidelity is yet to be revealed, at this stage. Although Birling also tells his daughter that she'll have to get used to it, her reply that she doesn't 'believe' she 'will' indicates her resistance to the dominant patriarchy. While I would commend her behaviour by 1912 standards, I would expect her to be much more outspoken in the face of sexual discrimination if it were to happen in a modern setting.

Birling's condescending and patronising tone is not simply reserved for women: his children are also victims in that sense. The fact that he talks over them indicates he doesn't listen to their views. When Eric tries to speak early on in the play, Birling continues in the same dominant vein, telling him: 'You've a lot to learn yet'. Priestley later shows us the irony in that statement, as it's Birling and his wife who learn the least after the Inspector's call. Priestley belief that younger people have more capability to learn from their mistakes than older people is exemplified by the older Birlings comparative lack of remorse at the end of the play. Of course, I would like to see the next generation make less mistakes than the previous one, but I'm not sure that will happen unless we work hard to make sure it does.

Comments

Drat! 912 words! All that painful cutting and I've still got more editing to do. Okay. Here's draft number 3.

3rd Draft

Birling lacks a social conscience, evidenced when he describes himself as 'a hard-headed businessman'. In short, Priestley allows Birling to give business a bad name, as he's dim-witted rather than 'hard-headed'. How could anyone respect Birling?

Indeed, Birling's predictions are continually lampooned through the use of dramatic irony. The audience has the benefit of hindsight and know the error inherent in other Birling statements, such as: 'Just because the miners came out on strike, there's a lot of wild talk about possible labour trouble'. Priestley and his audience knew of the General Strike of 1926. However, as much as Birling is ridiculed by the playwright, it is usually the business owners who win industrial disputes.

Like his prediction about future industrial unrest, Birling's belief in the Titanic's 'unsinkable' reputation is similarly misplaced. For Priestley, the ship represents the failings of big business, who put profits before the safety of passengers. Like Priestley, I believe that all lives are worth protecting, no matter what the cost.

Interestingly, the captain of the aforementioned Titanic, Edward Smith, may have agreed with Birling on many issues, given his last words were reputed to be: 'every man for himself'. This sentiment is echoed in the play by Birling, who says: 'a man [...] has to look after himself – and his family too'. As a committed socialist, Priestley would have frowned on this type of individualism or Social Darwinism. Likewise, while I believe individuals must look after themselves, I don't think it should be to the detriment of others.

Ironically, Birling himself is the victim of a similar kind of attitude. While he has married into the upper classes, his offspring, Sheila, is still not considered the equal of Gerald Croft. Birling says to Gerald: 'I have an idea that your mother -

Lady Croft - while she doesn't object to my girl - feels you might have done better for yourself socially'. While Priestley may not quite make the audience sympathise with Birling's character at this point, at least the playwright shows us that even the prejudiced can be victims of discrimination. While that does not justify discriminatory behaviour, it makes one realise how class warfare can be perpetuated.

Another form of prejudice rears its ugly head in the play, when Birling speaks of Russia. He clearly underestimates that nation's capabilities, referring to them as 'behindhand, naturally'. Priestley shows the audience that Birling's prejudice knows no bounds, which makes him a truly unsympathetic character. If we want to make the world a safer and better place to live, we have to try eliminate all forms of prejudice from our hearts and minds.

However, another form of prejudice exists within Birling: sexual discrimination. He tells Sheila that when she's married she'll 'realize that men with important work to do sometime have to spend nearly all their time and energy on business'. Ironically, Gerald, her fiancé, had been spending much of the last summer being unfaithful. Priestley, once again, makes the audience despise Birling's attitude; although Gerald's infidelity is yet to be revealed, at this stage. Although Birling also tells his daughter that she'll have to get used to it, her reply that she doesn't 'believe' she 'will' indicates her resistance to the dominant patriarchy. While I would commend her behaviour by 1912 standards, I would expect her to be much more outspoken in the face of sexual discrimination if it were to happen in a modern setting.

Birling's condescending and patronising tone is not simply reserved for women: his children are also victims. When Eric tries to speak early on in the play, Birling continues to dominate, saying: 'You've a lot to learn yet'. Priestley later shows us the irony in that statement, as it's Birling and his wife who learn the least after the Inspector's call. Priestley's belief that younger people have more capability to learn from their mistakes than older people is exemplified by the older Birlings' comparative lack of remorse at the end of the play. Of course, I would like to see the next generation make less mistakes than the previous one, but I'm not sure that will happen unless we work hard to make sure it does.

Comments

Wow! Still found a few mistakes, which I corrected. That's why you've got to keep editing. The good news is I'm down to 696 words now. That means I can use a 100 words on an introduction and a conclusion, so let's have a crack at that. First of all, I need to bring back my sub-titles.

Paragraph 1 - hard-headed businessman?

Paragraph 2 - miners

Paragraph 3 - The Titanic

Paragraph 4 - Social Darwinism

Paragraph 5 - social prejudice

Paragraph 6 - racism

Paragraph 7 - sexual discrimination

Paragraph 8 - ageism

I will incorporate all the above into my introduction. Here it goes:

Introduction

Social attitudes are examined in detail by Priestley in the play, particularly through the character of Birling, who represents an archetypal 1912 businessman. His attitudes towards the miners, The Titanic, family, class, race, gender and the younger generation will be each be explored in that order.

Comments

I had to change some of the paragraph headings to make it work, as I was discussing Birling's attitudes. However, I'm really pleased to tell the examiner what's coming up in this essay in less than 50 words! Now I've got more than 50 left for a conclusion. Once again, let's look at our paragraph headings and this time try to add the briefest concluding word(s) next to each of them.

Paragraph 1 - hard-headed businessman? - dim-witted

Paragraph 2 - miners - owners win

Paragraph 3 - The Titanic - profits put first

Paragraph 4 - Social Darwinism - family first

Paragraph 5 - social prejudice - victim of class

Paragraph 6 - racism - abuser

Paragraph 7 - sexual discrimination - abuser

Paragraph 8 - ageism - abuser

Birling is representative of the world's social evils: he embodies and promotes ageism, sexual discrimination, racism and class prejudice - although, he is also the victim of the latter. The audience are taken on a trip through history and we see the results of these vile and dim-witted points of view: the loss of life and dignity.

Comments

I wanted to write more, but I've restrained myself. That's 57 words for my conclusion. I've now got around 800 words for my assignment 3 for iGCSE and I'm a happy bunny!

Am I addressing the question of social attitudes? I think so. How about you? Check your work again!

Dramatisation of social attitudes: notes > PEE

Let's look at a few quotations from the text in note form and then convert those notes into PEE paragraphs about the dramatisation of social attitudes.

Notes

Point 1: Birling is interested in business and money. Portrayed as wealthy, without much concern for employees. Lacks a social conscience.

Evidence/Quotation 1: 'There's a good deal of silly talk about [...] I speak as a hard-headed business man [...] ignore all this silly pessimistic talk'

Explanation 1: JBP doesn't agree with Arthur Birling. Shows it through dramatic irony when Birling predicts a prosperous & peaceful future, before Great Depression & WW1. JBP's arguing in favour of collective responsibility.

So that's what the notes look like. Let's convert those notes into a PEE paragraph.

Finished PEE paragraph

Birling seems interested in business and money mainly. He is generally portrayed as wealthy, without much concern for his employees. He appears to lack a social conscience and this is exemplified when he says: 'There's a good deal of silly talk about [...] I speak as a hard-headed business man [...] ignore all this silly pessimistic talk'. He seems proud of himself and it's clear that the playwright is setting Birling up for a fool to discredit Birling's views. J.B. Priestley does this effectively through the use of dramatic irony, as the 'pessimistic talk' that Birling refers to is quite accurate with the benefit of historical hindsight. The play is set just before World War One and the Great Depression that followed a decade or so afterwards. Additionally, the playwright makes Birling appear to be pompous and dismissive of other points of view, which the character describes as 'silly'. Priestley does not want his audience to sympathise with this character, who is a capitalist and would therefore be completely opposed to the playwright's brand of socialism and collective responsibility.

Okay, I'll be honest! I'm not expecting you to write that much for each quotation you use. By the way, 'quotation' is a noun and 'quote' is a verb. Some markers may be sticklers for accuracy, so I suggest you can quotations exactly that! Even if your teachers insists that anything that appears within quotation marks is a quote. If that were true, wouldn't they be called 'quote marks'? Forgive me, I digress!

What you should be writing for a PEE paragraph is a minimum of 3 sentences. I'd aim for about 4 or 5 generally, as you need to really explain the relevance of your quotation and refer back to the question to make sure you're on track. It's very easy to go off at a tangent, so by referring back to the question in the last sentence of each paragraph you can ensure that you stay on task.

Page-by-page analysis

The scenery in Act One suggests a lack of family warmth and homeliness, as the stage directions describe the scene as 'not cosy and homelike' (p161). Immediately, the audience get the idea that all is not what it seems in this environment. However, the lighting is 'pink and intimate until the inspector arrives' so at least there is a semblance of a normal home life (161). When the inspector arrives the light becomes 'brighter and harder', showing that the truth is not always pleasant (161).

We also discover that the house has all the trappings of a prosperous and extravagant lifestyle, judging by the 'champagne glasses', 'decanter of port, cigar box and cigarettes' (161).

Arthur Birling is revealed to be 'rather provincial in his speech (161). This shows that he is upwardly mobile with possible delusions of grandeur, seeing as he is described as 'portentous', or pompous (161). He was not born to wealth, unlike his wife, Sybil.

Mrs Birling is described as 'her husband's social superior', which confirms that by marrying Arthur has moved up a class (161).

Their children are Eric and Sheila, both in their 20s. Eric is described as 'half shy, half assertive', which lets the audience know that there are two sides at least to his character (161). Sheila, meanwhile, seems one-dimensional in comparison, as she is 'pretty' and 'very pleased with life'(161).

Gerald Croft seems to be a bit of a playboy, as he is described as a 'young man-about-town' (161).

We realise very quickly that the group are celebrating something, and the first whiff we get something not being quite right is when Sheila says to Gerald half-playfully that he'never came near' her during last summer (162). Bearing in mind they are getting engaged, this does seem a little strange.

However, Mrs Birling backs up Gerald's excuse that he was busy at work by saying: 'when you're married you'll realise that men with important work to do sometimes have to spend nearly all their time and energy on their business' (163). Immediately, we discover that Sheila has a different attitude to men compared to her mother, who seems more ready to play a traditional role. The suggestion is that Sheila has a more rebellious nature than her mother.

Eric's lack of control is evident when he 'suddenly guffaws' (163). His laugh puts him at odds with his sister, as he is mocking Gerald. At this stage, the two siblings are not exactly getting on.

We get the idea that Mr Birling is not truly accepted as a member of the aristocracy, as Gerald's parents have not attended the engagement party. They have made the excuse that they are abroad, but Mr Birling take solace in the fact he has received 'a very nice cable', or in other words a message, from Sir George and Lady Croft (163).

We quickly find out Mr Birling has intentions of joining his company with that of Gerald's parents to bring about 'lower costs and higher prices'(164). Immediately, it seems that Priestley is portraying Mr Birling at worst kind of capitalist, without social conscience. Lower costs mean low wages for employees and higher prices mean the exploitation of the consumer.

Mr Birling plays his cards on the table metaphorically, revealing that he believes that entrepreneurial risk should be rewarded. Priestley uses dramatic irony to mock Birling's point of view, as he tells his prospective son-in-law that he 'can ignore all this silly pessimistic talk' (165). Birling claims that the 'worst' of the miners strikes are over, yet in the following decade a general strike cripples the country. He also predicts 'a time of increasing prosperity' (165). That is also ludicrous as the Great Depression of the 1930s rocked the world economy. Birling goes on to make himself even more foolish by saying: 'The Germans don't want war' (165). The play is set in 1912, just two years before the commencement of the First World War.

Making himself look even more foolish, Birling describes the *Titanic* as 'absolutely unsinkable' (166). Of course, we know with hindsight that the ship sank in April 1912, and the audience that watched the play being performed for the first time in 1946 would have known that also. This is of course another example of dramatic irony and to cap it all off, Birling mentions that Russia 'will always be behindhand' (166). This is also ridiculous, as Russia made rapid progress after the Russian Revolution of 1917.

Birling also criticises socialist writers, such as George Bernard Shaw and H.G. Wells. He says: 'We can't let these [...] do all the talking' (166). Clearly, Birling is on the right wing of the political spectrum.

It is obvious that Lady Croft does not accept the Birlings as a social equal, as revealed when Arthur tells Gerald that his mother 'feels you might have done better to yourself socially' (167). Nevertheless, Birling feels it's only a matter of time before he gets 'a knighthood' , adding ominously 'so long as we behave ourselves' (167).

Birling continues to talk about his philosophy, saying that 'a man has to make his own way - has to look after himself -and his family too' (168). He rejects the idea that people are 'like bees in a hive' so feels no sense of social responsibility for others' welfare (168).

When the Inspector arrives, Birling brags that he 'was an alderman for years - and Lord Mayor two years ago' (169). Birling seems to have the upper hand, at this stage, as he also mentions that he knows 'the Brumley police officers pretty well' and has never seen the Inspector before (169).

Priestley uses dramatic devices to change the balance of power. The Inspector asserts himself through his use of superior knowledge. He tells them that 'a young woman died' through swallowing disinfectant (170). He also mentions that 'a letter', 'a sort of diary' and a 'photograph' had been found (170). The other characters seem less confident after this revelation.

Birling is the first to be interrogated and he readily admits that the dead woman, Eva Smith, was one of his employees. Ironically, Birling claims 'there's nothing mysterious - or scandalous - about this business' (171).

However, through the inspectors questioning we find out the Birling began the chain of events that ended Eva's life. Birling replies that he 'can't except any responsibility', which is in keeping with his philosophy that everyone should look after themselves (172).

Despite this, Birling does go on to reveal more about Eva. He tells how she was 'a good worker', but asking for higher wages did not go down well with the management (172). Birling wanted to keep 'labour costs down', but Eva and the other workers went on strike (173). Birling thought that Eva was one of the 'ringleaders', so fired her (173).

Eric's attitude to the story shows that he has a sensitive side, calling it 'tough luck' (173). Birling is not impressed with the Inspector's attitude, so asks him his name. The Inspector spells out his surname: 'Goole' (173). This, of course, makes the audience think that the Inspector could in fact be a ghost. Meanwhile, Birling is still not quite convinced by the Inspector's identity, as he asks him if he knows his friend, 'Chief Constable, Colonel Roberts' (173). The Inspector's reply that he doesn't 'see much of him' suggests that he has a lowly status in the police force.

Interestingly, Birling criticises his son, Eric, for exactly the same thing he is guilty of: lacking responsibility. Priestley uses irony to emphasise Birling's ignorance when he says: 'It's about time you learn to face a few responsibilities' (174). The reason why Birling attacked his son is because Eric is the belief that Eva Smith is entitled to 'try for higher wages' (174).

Birling maintains he was 'justified' in sacking Eva, for she 'had been causing trouble in the works' (175). Gerald, agrees with his prospective father-in-law much to the consternation of Sheila, who says: 'I can't help thinking about this girl' (175). Like a brother, Eric, Sheila is a character showing a sense of conscience, quite in contrast with the nonchalant attitude displayed by Birling and Gerald.

Sheila gets the idea that the Inspector is talking as if they 'were responsible' for the death of Eva Smith (176). It appears that unlike her father and her prospective husband, she is actually listening to what the Inspector is saying and not dismissing Eva Smith's death as something inconsequential.

Likewise, her brother Eric has sympathy for Eva, as he says: 'Can't blame her' when we find out she changed the name after Mr Birling sacked her (176). The Inspector explains that many young women are desperate and are consequently used 'for cheap labour' (177). Once again, Sheila voices her sympathy by saying: 'these girls aren't cheap labour - their *people*' (177). This reveals Sheila's social conscience and her awareness that women need greater equality.

We then come across one of the dramatic devices that affects characters immediately. The device in question is 'the photograph' (178). The use of dramatic devices like these helps build a chain of events which has resulted in *An Inspector Calls* being described as a 'well-made play'.

Anyway, the photograph results in Sheila literally running away from her responsibilities, as she 'gives a half-stifled sob, and then runs out' (178).

Birling then shows his patronising and protective side, still showing no sympathy for Eva at all, by saying to the Inspector: 'Why the devil do you want to go upsetting the child like that?' (178).

When she returns she begins to take some responsibility for the death of Eva Smith, by saying: 'So I'm really responsible?' (179). The Inspector answers the question by saying that she is 'partly to blame' (180). He reminds her that her father is too.

Sheila then relates the story, which shows how envious she was of Eva, who was extremely 'pretty' (180). Sheila was guilty of petty spite as she 'went to the manager and told him that this girl had been very impertinent' (180). This, of course, led to Eva being sacked moving her closer to her ultimate downfall.

Sheila shows remorse and says: 'I'll never, never do it again to anybody' (181). The focus of the investigation moves to Gerald, as the Inspector reveals that Eva Smith 'changed her name to Daisy Renton' (181).

Before Gerald is interrogated, he has a private moment with Sheila when it is clear that he wants to maintain the deceit.

Gerald's statement: 'We can keep it from him' gets the following reply from Sheila: 'Why - you fool - *he knows*. Of course he knows' (182). Gerald is described as looking 'crushed' and his self-assurance at the start of the play is now gone. There seems to be a major shift in power at this point at the end of Act One, as the Inspector has now taken on the role of an all-knowing inquisitor. He is suddenly an almost godlike figure, judging the characters.

Act Two

Gerald reveals his chauvinist nature, by trying to excuse his wife-to-be from the room by saying: 'she's obviously had about as much as she can stand' (183). Prior to that, he had talked about her as if she were a child, by saying: 'She's had a long, exciting and tiring day' (183). Sheila stands up for her rights, by insisting on staying put. The Inspector shows how hypocritical Gerald is by asking him: 'And you think young women ought to be protected against unpleasant and disturbing things?' (183). Gerald replies: 'If possible - yes' (183). Of course, given his treatment of Daisy Renton that we are about to hear about, we may think he should practice what he preaches.

The Inspector clearly believes that the 'guilt' for the death should be shared (184). Sheila keeps reiterating how 'sorry' she is (184). At this part of the play, she is at loggerheads with Gerald who accuses her of wanting 'to see somebody else put through' the Inspector's interrogation (184). That is one thing, she claims to not be guilty of, although she admits getting Eva sacked was 'selfish' and 'vindictive' (184).

Sheila is incredibly critical of her mother, Mrs Birling, who enters the room 'briskly and self-confidently' (185). She is blissfully unaware of all the accusations have taken place. Sheila tells her mother that she is 'beginning all wrong' (185).

Mrs Birling belittles her daughter by saying to the Inspector: 'You seem to have made a great impression on this child' (185). She tries the same trick as Gerald to get Sheila out of the room, saying: 'You're looking tired, dear. I think you ought to go to bed' (185). It appears that despite Sheila's forthcoming marriage, Mrs Birling does not see her daughter as a fully grown adult yet. Her patronising tone makes Mrs Birling's portrayal very unsympathetic to a watching audience.

Mrs Birling's prejudice for working-class girls is revealed quickly as she claims they can't possibly 'understand why the girl committed suicide' given the class she is from (185-6). Sheila takes umbrage at her mother's use of the word 'impertinent' to describe the Inspector. This same word has been used by Sheila to describe Eva Smith. There is more wordplay between the Inspector and Mrs Birling over 'offence', which could be meant in the criminal sense but isn't here.

The next revelation is Eric's alcoholism. Gerald reveals that he has 'gathered' that Eric 'does drink pretty hard' (187). Perhaps Gerald is trying to deflect some of the blame away from himself before he begins his account of his affair with Daisy Renton.

After being asked, by the Inspector directly, Gerald begins to reveal the story behind this relationship with Daisy (which is, of course, a worthless, cheap but pretty weed). Gerald says they met in March 1911 in the 'Palace music hall' (188).

Gerald describes that place as 'a favourite haunt of women of the town' (189). This phrase is a polite euphemism for prostitutes. It also indicates that despite his reputation in polite society, Gerald is quite willing to spend his time in places of ill-repute. However, Daisy was unlike the 'hard-eyed dough-faced women' that would normally be found in such a place (189). Gerald admits that Daisy was not enjoying herself, with 'Old Joe Meggarty' wetting her 'into a corner' (189). Mrs Birling is astounded that Gerald is talking about 'Alderman Meggarty' (189). The name Meggarty sounds like 'maggoty' and therefore adds to the disgust that the audience must feel at this account.

To make it worse, Gerald describes Meggarty as 'one of the worst sots and rogues in Brumley' (190). Of course, by being a drunken sot, Meggarty is comparable to Eric. Gerald believes he did the right thing in rescuing her when he noticed her 'looking' his way (190). He saw it as 'a cry for help' (190).

Gerald admits that he gave Eva money and put her in his friends 'nice little set of rooms' (191). He claims that he 'didn't ask for anything in return' (191). He says it was 'inevitable' that she became his mistress (191). This indicates that Gerald is very reluctant to take on responsibility for his actions.

Sheila mocks her fiance, calling him 'the wonderful Fairy Prince' (192). She does praise him for being 'honest', and she is growing in power at this stage of the play (192).

Mrs Birling describes Gerald's fling, which happened from March until September 1911, as a 'disgusting affair' (192). Gerald refutes this, saying: 'it wasn't disgusting' (192). At the time, it was frowned upon for upper-class people to have much to do with the lower classes, of which Eva was a member.

After these revelations, Sheila 'hands' Gerald back his engagement ring (193). Gerald is allowed to go for a walk by the Inspector, who reveals that Eva then went to the seaside for a couple of months (according to her diary).

Just before Gerald goes, Sheila tells him that she respects him 'more', partly because of his honesty (194). It seems like she has not given up the idea of marriage to him.

Mr Birling wants to sweep the whole affair under the carpet, it seems, but Sheila cuts him off when he says: But you must understand that a lot of young men -' (194). Sheila has assumed more power as the players gone on, and even Gerald claims he knows what she means when she says they will 'have to start all over again' (194). Gerald seems to learn something from the experience, whereas Mr Birling seems to be the same as he was the star of the play.

We find out that the Inspector didn't show the photograph to Gerald. Therefore, the audience may believe that Daisy Renton is in fact a different girl. However, he does show the photograph to Mrs Birling, who claims that she doesn't recognise the girl.

The Inspector reminds Birling, who interrupts, that public men 'have responsibilities as well as privileges'. The inspector has an ally in Sheila, who is now acting like his sidekick. Class means little to Sheila now as she tells her mother and father that 'we've no excuse now putting on airs' (195).

With Birling out of the room, the Inspector asks Mrs Birling if she is a prominent member 'of the Brumley Women's Charity Organization' (195). She admits she is an claims that they have done 'a great deal of useful work in helping deserving cases' (195). This is quite ironic given what we are about to find out.

Under pressure, and with her husband back in the room, Mrs Birling reveals that a pregnant Eva Smith 'appealed' to her organisation for help (196). However, the appeal was not under the name Eva Smith, nor was it under Daisy Renton. Mrs Birling says that Eva called herself 'Mrs Birling' (197). She admits that 'that was one of the things that prejudiced me against her case' (197). Mrs Birling refused to help Eva and shows no remorse when she says: 'I consider I did my duty' (197).

Ironically, given what we are about to find out, Mrs Birling says: 'Go and look for the father of the child. It is his responsibility' (198). Sheila condemns her mother calling her lack of action: 'cruel and vile' (198).

Mrs Birling says that Eva described the father as 'only a youngster - see the wild and drinking too much' (199). Even told her that she had received money from the young man, but didn't want to take any more from him. It was out of the question for her to marry him, as it 'would be wrong for them both' (199). Mrs Birling says that it was ridiculous to believe that 'a girl of that sort would ever refuse money' (199). This shows her contempt of the lower classes. It also shows that she is too blind to see that Eric fits the description of the man whose baby Eva was carrying.

Mrs Birling says that she accepts 'no blame for it at all' (200). She says the girl and 'the young man who was the father of the child she was going to have' are to blame (200). She adds that if Eva's story was true, that the father of the child was stealing money, then 'he'd be entirely responsible' (200). Again, Mrs Birling fails to see the similarity between the young man in question and her own son, Eric.

Mrs Birling continues to adopt a patronising tone, telling her daughter that she is 'behaving like an hysterical child' (201). Sheila was trying to warn her mother of the implications of what she was saying and, now at the end of Act Two, she realises that her son may have been the father of the unborn child. The Inspector has made Mrs Birling 'frightened' and Mr Birling 'terrified', with Eric entering the room 'looking extremely pale and distressed' (201). This is quite a cliffhanger check end Act Two with.

Act Three

Eric is in the spotlight, waiting for the interrogation to come, but his mother still insists: 'I didn't know it was you - I never dreamt. Besides, you're not that type - you don't get drunk ' (202). This speech shows how little she knows about her own son.

The Inspector insists that Eric 'needs a drink now just see him through' and his father reluctantly allows it (July 3). From the way that Eric handles 'the decanter and then the drink' with 'familiarity' it is obvious that he is a heavy drinker (203).

Eric admits that he met Eva in November 1911 in the Palace bar. Like Gerald, Eric says that Eva 'wasn't the usual sort' (203). Nevertheless, he treats her like a cheap prostitute forcing himself upon her, while trying to justify his actions by saying he 'was in that state when a chap easily turns nasty' (203).

Eric shows his shallowness by saying that he 'wasn't in love with her or anything', despite admitting that they 'made love again' (204). Like Gerald, he tries to deflect some blame from himself by saying how much he hates the 'fat old tarts round the town' that he sees his father's friends associating with (204).

Eric seems quite selfish when asked about how worried Eva was about being pregnant. Eric replies: 'I was in a hell of a state about it' (204). He can only see his own point of view.

Eric admits that he took money from his father's 'office', but when asked if he stole it he says: 'Not really' (205). This shows that Eric is immature and lacks a sense of responsibility. He cannot own not for what he's done entirely. And yet he's entirely to blame, according to his mother, who said that before she knew the identity of the father of the unborn child.

Eric says he 'intended to pay it back' and therefore taking money does not amount to stealing (205). He reveals that his relationship with his father is weak, for when Birling asks him why he didn't come to him he replies: 'you're not the kind of father a chap could go to when he's in trouble' (205).

Eric confirms that either would not take stole the money and then he launches into an attack on his mother, saying: 'you killed her - and the child she'd have had too - my child - your own grandchild' (206). After this outburst, Mrs Birling finally shows a measure of remorse. Perhaps she has now realised that interconnectedness of the world. The Inspector refuses to apportion blame to one person, saying: 'each of you helped to kill her' (206). The Inspector then uses a simile to condemn how Eric used Eva 'as if she was an animal, a thing, not a person' (207).

Before leaving, the Inspector makes didactic, polemic final speech. He is as moralistic as a preacher as he says: 'We are members of one body. We are responsible for each other' (207). He warns that if humankind do not learn that simple lesson that 'they will be taught it in fire and blood and anguish' (207). The only character who has emerged with any credit at all it seems in the Inspector's eyes is Gerald, who 'at least had some affection for her and made her happy for a time' (207).

After he leaves, the family begin to blame each other, with Birling turning on his son saying: 'You're the one I blame for this' (207). It seems Birling has learnt nothing from the Inspector's visit, as he can't accept his own part in Eva's death.

All Birling can think of is that he was 'almost certain for a knighthood in the next Honours List' (208). This shows his only concerned about prestige. He wants to punish Eric, by making him 'work for nothing' (208). Working for close-to-nothing is what drove Eva to her death, a point that Birling has not understood. Sheila has picked this up, as she says: 'you don't seem to learn anything' (208).

Sheila wonders if the Inspector really was 'a police officer' (209). Nevertheless, she's decided to take on board what he said, unlike her father, who disagrees. She describes her parents as 'childish - trying not to face the facts' (209).

Mrs Birling claims that the Inspector didn't make her 'confess' (210). Her husband agrees, saying that Eric and Sheila allowed themselves 'to be bluffed' (210). There is now a clear division between parents and children, with the latter accepting more responsibility and guilt than the former.

Mrs Birling tries to quieten Eric and Sheila by telling them to 'just be quiet so that your father can decide what we ought to do' (211). Clearly, Mrs Birling is happy to play second fiddle to her husband to re-establish the status quo.

Gerald returns and confirms what Sheila believed that the Inspector 'wasn't a police officer' (212). Mr Birling phones his friend in the police force, Colonel Roberts, and confirms it.

Mr Birling and Gerald think that this revelation 'makes all the difference', which is a sentiment that Sheila and Eric disagree with (213). Sheila forgives Gerald mistake, as he didn't hear everyone's confession. Meanwhile, Birling tries to dismiss the Inspector's visit as a hoax.

Eric finally admits his guilt, when it comes to the stolen money, but he sees the bigger picture when he says: 'The money's not the important thing. It's what happens at the girl and what we will did to her that matters' (214).

Gerald still disagrees that they are responsible for driving the girl to suicide. He says: 'Did we? Who says so? Because I say - there is no more real evidence we did then there was that that was a police inspector' (215).

Gerald then points out something perhaps they not thought of. He asks them: 'How do you know it's the same girl?' (216). He reminds them that he didn't look at the photograph and that none of them saw it at the same time. Gerald is ready to dismiss it all as 'nonsense' rather than focusing on the idea that they are all guilty of something (217). Just to prove once and for all the Inspector is a fraud, Gerald decides to call the infirmary to find out if they have 'had a goal brought in this afternoon who committed suicide by drinking disinfectant' (218).

Birling is delighted to find out that the 'story's just a lot moonshine' (219). The word 'moonshine' can refer to alcohol, which is ironic given that it was Eric's drunken advances that caused Eva to become pregnant.

The final dramatic device appears at the end of the play, as 'the telephone rings sharply'. Birling reveals that 'it was the police' and that 'a girl has just died' (220). An inspector is on the way to ask them questions, which shows there is every likelihood they will have to make the same revelations once more. Perhaps, the younger generation will admit their guilt more quickly this time, as the audience contemplate the unanswered question: who was the Inspector? A ghost, Eva Smith's father or someone or something else.

Essay writing tips

<u>Use a variety of connectives</u>

Have a look of this list of connectives. Which of these would you choose to use?

'ADDING' DISCOURSE MARKERS

- AND

- ALSO

- AS WELL AS

- MOREOVER

- TOO

- FURTHERMORE

- ADDITIONALLY

I hope you chose 'additionally', 'furthermore' and 'moreover'. Don't be afraid to use the lesser discourse markers, as they are also useful. Just avoid using those ones over and over again. I've seen essays from Key Stage 4 students that use the same discourse marker for the opening sentence of each paragraph! Needless to say, those essays didn't get great marks!

Okay, here are some more connectives for you to look at. Select the best ones.

'SEQUENCING' DISCOURSE MARKERS

- NEXT

- FIRSTLY

- SECONDLY

- THIRDLY

- FINALLY

- MEANWHILE

- AFTER

- THEN

- SUBSEQUENTLY

This time, I hope you chose 'subsequently' and 'meanwhile'.

Here are some more connectives for you to 'grade'!

'ILLUSTRATING / EXEMPLIFYING' DISCOURSE MARKERS

- FOR EXAMPLE

- SUCH AS

- FOR INSTANCE

- IN THE CASE OF

- AS REVEALED BY

- ILLUSTRATED BY

I'd probably go for 'illustrated by' or even 'as exemplified by' (which is not in the list!). Please feel free to add your own examples to the lists. Strong connectives impress examiners. Don't forget it! That's why I want you to look at some more.

'CAUSE & EFFECT' DISCOURSE MARKERS

- BECAUSE

- SO

- THEREFORE

- THUS

- CONSEQUENTLY

- HENCE

I'm going for 'consequently' this time. How about you? What about the next batch?

'COMPARING' DISCOURSE MARKERS

- SIMILARLY

- LIKEWISE

- AS WITH

- LIKE

- EQUALLY

- IN THE SAME WAY

I'd choose 'similarly' this time. Still some more to go.

'QUALIFYING' DISCOURSE MARKERS

- BUT
- HOWEVER
- WHILE
- ALTHOUGH
- UNLESS
- EXCEPT
- APART FROM
- AS LONG AS

It's 'however' for me!

'CONTRASTING' DISCOURSE MARKERS

- WHEREAS
- INSTEAD OF
- ALTERNATIVELY
- OTHERWISE
- UNLIKE
- ON THE OTHER HAND

- CONVERSELY

I'll take 'conversely' or 'alternatively' this time.

'EMPHASISING' DISCOURSE MARKERS

- ABOVE ALL

- IN PARTICULAR

- ESPECIALLY

- SIGNIFICANTLY

- INDEED

- NOTABLY

You can breathe a sigh of relief now! It's over! No more connectives. However, now I want to put our new-found skills to use in our essays.

Useful information/Glossary

Allegory: extended metaphor, like the grim reaper representing death, e.g. Scrooge symbolizing capitalism.

Alliteration: same consonant sound repeating, e.g. 'She sells sea shells'.

Allusion: reference to another text/person/place/event.

Ascending tricolon: sentence with three parts, each increasing in power, e.g. 'ringing, drumming, shouting'.

Aside: character speaking so some characters cannot hear what is being said. Sometimes, an aside is directly to the audience. It's a dramatic technique which reveals the character's inner thoughts and feelings.

Assonance: same vowel sounds repeating, e.g. 'Oh no, won't Joe go?'

Bathos: abrupt change from sublime to ridiculous for humorous effect.

Blank verse: lines of unrhymed iambic pentameter.

Compressed time: when the narrative is fast-forwarding through the action.

Descending tricolon: sentence with three parts, each decreasing in power, e.g. 'shouting, talking, whispering'.

Denouement: tying up loose ends, the resolution.

Diction: choice of words or vocabulary.

Didactic: used to describe literature designed to inform, instruct or pass on a moral message.

Dilated time: opposite compressed time, here the narrative is in slow motion.

Direct address: second person narrative, predominantly using the personal pronoun 'you'.

Dramatic action verb: manifests itself in physical action, e.g. I punched him in the face.

Dramatic irony: audience knows something that the character is unaware of.

Ellipsis: leaving out part of the story and allowing the reader to fill in the narrative gap.

End-stopped lines: poetic lines that end with punctuation.

Epistolary: letter or correspondence-driven narrative.

Flashback/Analepsis: going back in time to the past, interrupting the chronological sequence.

Flashforward/Prolepsis: going forward in time to the future, interrupting the chronological sequence.

Foreshadowing/Adumbrating: suggestion of plot developments that will occur later in the narrative.

Gothic: another strand of Romanticism, typically with a wild setting, a sensitive heroine, an older man with a 'piercing gaze', discontinuous structure, doppelgangers, guilt and the 'unspeakable' (according to Eve Kosofsky Sedgwick).

Hamartia: character flaw, leading to that character's downfall.

Hyperbole: exaggeration for effect.

Iambic pentameter: a line of ten syllables beginning with a lighter stress alternating with a heavier stress in its perfect form, which sounds like a heartbeat. The stress falls on the even syllables, numbers: 2, 4, 6, 8 and 10, e.g. 'When now I think you can behold such sights'.

Intertextuality: links to other literary texts.

Irony: amusing or cruel reversal of expected outcome or words meaning the opposite to their literal meaning.

Metafiction/Romantic irony: self-conscious exposure of the devices used to create 'the truth' within a work of fiction.

Motif: recurring image use of language or idea that connects the narrative together and creates a theme or mood, e.g. 'green light' in *The Great Gatsby.*

Oxymoron: contradictory terms combined, e.g. deafening silence.

Pastiche: imitation of another's work.

Pathetic fallacy: a form of personification whereby inanimate objects show human attributes, e.g. 'the sea smiled benignly'.

The originator of the term, John Ruskin in 1856, used 'the cruel, crawling foam', from Kingsley's *The Sands of Dee*, as an example to clarify what he meant by the 'morbid' nature of pathetic fallacy.

Personification: concrete or abstract object made human, often simply achieved by using a capital letter or a personal pronoun, e.g. 'Nature', or describing a ship as 'she'.

Pun/Double entendre: a word with a double meaning, usually employed in witty wordplay but not always.

Retrospective: account of events after they have occurred.

Romanticism: genre celebrating the power of imagination, spriritualism and nature.

Semantic/lexical field: related words about a single concept, e.g. king, queen and prince are all concerned with royalty.

Soliloquy: character thinks aloud, but is not heard by other characters (unlike in a monologue) giving the audience access to inner thoughts and feelings.

Style: choice of language, form and structure, and effects produced.

Synecdoche: one part of something referring to the whole, e.g. Carker's teeth represent him in *Dombey and Son*.

Syntax: the way words and sentences are placed together.

Tetracolon climax: sentence with four parts, culminating with the last part, e.g. 'I have nothing to offer but blood, toil, tears, and sweat ' (Winston Churchill).

ABOUT THE AUTHOR

Joe Broadfoot is a secondary school teacher of English and a soccer journalist, who also writes fiction and literary criticism. His former experiences as a DJ took him to far-flung places such as Tokyo, Kobe, Beijing, Hong Kong, Jakarta, Cairo, Dubai, Cannes, Oslo, Bergen and Bodo. He is now PGCE and CELTA-qualified with QTS, a first-class honours degree in Literature and an MA in Victorian Studies (majoring in Charles Dickens). Drama is close to his heart as he acted in 'Macbeth' and 'A Midsummer Night's Dream' at the Royal Northern College of Music in Manchester. More recently, he has been teaching 'Much Ado About Nothing' to 'A' Level students at a secondary school in Buckinghamshire, 'An Inspector Calls' at a school in west London 'Heroes' at a school in Kent and 'A Christmas Carol' at a school in south London.

13180189R00032

Printed in Great Britain
by Amazon.co.uk, Ltd.,
Marston Gate.